DATE DUE

THE EMPIRE OF MALI

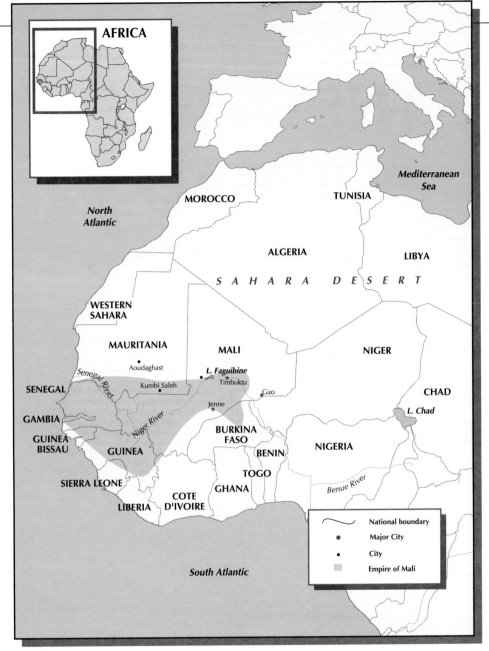

The Empire of Mali was one of the largest and best-known empires in history.

~African Civilizations~

THE EMPIRE OF MALI

Carol Thompson

A First Book

Franklin Watts
A Division of Grolier Publishing
New York / London / Hong Kong / Sydney
Danbury, Connecticut

Cover photograph copyright ©: The Cleveland Museum of Art

Photographs copyright ©: M. Ascani/Liaison International: p. 7; Marc Deville/Gamma Liaison: pp. 9, 14; A. Lorgnier/Visa/Gamma Liaison: p. 10; Carol Thompson: pp. 12, 33, 36; Werner Forman Archive: pp. 16, 24; Xavier Rossi/Gamma Liaison: p. 19; Trip/Trip/Viesti Collection: pp. 23, 41; Wolfgang Kaehler/Liaison International: p. 25; Trip/M. Jelliffe/Viesti Associates, Inc.: p. 27; Trip/Trip/Viesti Associates, Inc.: p. 31; Wolfgang Kaehler/Corbis: p. 34; Charles and Josette Lenars/Corbis: pp. 43, 48; Yves Bresson/Gamma Liaison: p. 45; Michel Renaudeau/Liaison International: p. 50; Pierre Perrin/Gamma Liaison: p. 52; Map Division, The New York Public Library, Astor, Lenox and Tilden Foundations: p. 54; Robert Thompson: p. 57.

Library of Congress Cataloging-in-Publication Data

Thompson, Carol (Carol Ann)
    The empire of Mali / by Carol Thompson.
        p.   cm. — (African civilizations)
    Includes bibliographical references (p.   ) and index.
    ISBN 0-531-20277-1
    1. Mali (Empire)—History—Juvenile literature.   I. Title.
    II. Series
    DT532.2.T47   1998
    966.2'017—dc21   97-37353
                                                      CIP
                                                      AC

Copyright © 1998 by The Rosen Publishing Group, Inc.
All rights reserved. Published simultaneously in Canada
Printed in the United States of America
1 2 3 4 5 6 7 8 9 10 R 05 04 03 02 01 00 99 98

CONTENTS

INTRODUCTION

The Empire of Mali was one of the largest empires the world has ever known. It flourished in West Africa from A.D. 1235 until 1464.

The Empire of Mali was located in the *Sahel*, a dry grassland region that lies between the Sahara Desert to the north and forest regions to the south. In the forests, close to the source of the Niger River, were the rich gold mines of Bambuk and Bure. Wealthy cities of the Mediterranean lay to the north, beyond the Sahara.

Located between these two sources of wealth, the Sahel was ideally placed to become a trading center for goods from both regions. As a result, several trading cities developed in this region. They became rich and powerful by taxing all the products traded in their territory.

For centuries, camel caravans have carried trade goods across the Sahara Desert.

The traders from the north and east who crossed the Sahara Desert on camels were mostly Berbers, desert peoples who followed several different Islamic *sects*. The most precious product loaded onto their camels was salt, which they traded for gold. Salt was worth its weight in gold because even small amounts are essential for a healthful diet, particularly in the hot climates of the Sahara. In addition to gold and salt, many other goods were traded in the Sahel, including slaves, ivory, animal skins from the south, and luxury products from the Mediterranean and the East.

The vast trade networks and the major cities of the Sahel were first controlled by the Empire of Ghana, which collapsed 150 years before the Empire of Mali rose to power. The Empire of Ghana was weakened because many of its leaders began to compete for power. The empire's trade links were also damaged by fighting among the various Berber groups. Finally, the Almoravid Berbers from Morocco defeated the Empire of Ghana in 1076. The empire fell into chaos because minor kings, all of whom had been part of the empire, competed for control. The king who emerged as the strongest was Sumanguru, king of the Susu people.

Sumanguru was in turn conquered by Sundiata, who ruled the small Kingdom of Mali. A great leader and skillful *negotiator*, Sundiata reunited the peoples of the region. Following the recipe for success that had made the Empire of Ghana a great trading state, Sundiata restored trade and created the Empire of Mali.

The Empire of Mali enjoyed peace and prosperity, and its cities, including Niani, Jenne, Walata,

A Berber in Morocco

Market day at Jenne, with its famous mosque in the background

Timbuktu, and Gao, became famous as centers of trade, culture, and learning. At the height of its power, the Empire of Mali stretched almost 2,000 miles (3,200 km) from west to east, from the Atlantic Ocean in the west to beyond Gao in the east, and from the southern edge of the Sahara to the forest belt in the south. It was one of the richest and largest empires the world has ever seen, and its fame spread through Europe, Arabia, and Asia.

The Empire of Mali flourished until the second half of the fifteenth century, when it started to decline. Finally, by the end of the sixteenth century, the empire was reduced to a small *city-state.*

1 MALI BEFORE THE EMPIRE

The Empire of Mali—like the Empire of Ghana—was built by Mande-speaking peoples who spoke similar languages and shared a common culture. Ghana was built by the Soninke; the Empire of Mali was built by the *Mandinka* people (also known as Malinke or Mandingo). Other peoples who contributed to the rise of the Empire of Mali included Berber traders (such as the Tuareg), Fulbe (or Fulani) herdsmen, Arab merchants and scholars, and Bozo, Somono, and Sorko fishermen.

The Mandinka word *mali* means "hippopotamus," but it eventually came to mean "the place where the king lives." One Malian legend describes

Mandinka boys from present-day Mali

how Sundiata, who enlarged the small Kingdom of Mali into an enormous empire, changed himself into a hippopotamus in the Sankarani River.

SOURCES OF HISTORY

Information on the history of the Empire of Mali comes from early accounts by Arab writers; archaeologists, scientists who study how people lived long ago; and the stories of *griots*, the people who have traditionally learned and taught history in West Africa. Griots memorize long historical accounts, or epics, and pass them on from generation to generation by word of mouth. They use music, poetry, drama, and dance to both entertain and teach. Griots play a stringed instrument called a *kora*. With their *koras* and songs, griots challenge and inspire their listeners to match or surpass the heroic deeds of their ancestors.

Griots also had important political and administrative roles in the Empire of Mali. They defended the empire's constitution and its legal principles, and they served as advisors to kings and as tutors to princes.

A modern-day griot from Mali named Djeli

Throughout West Africa songs are an important way of recalling the past and teaching history.

Mamoudou Kouyate, describes his role this way in the book *Sundiata* by D. T. Niane: "Since time immemorial, my family has been in the service of the princes of Mali. I teach kings the history of their ancestors so that the lives of the ancients might serve them as an example, for the world is old, but the future springs from the past. Whoever knows the history of a country can read its future."

THE FIRST KING OF MALI

Mandinka history describes how, before the founding of the Mali Empire, the Mandinka were divided into twelve clans, each made up of hunters, blacksmiths, or artisans. Each clan had its own king, and they were often at war with one another. To end the conflict, the twelve kings formed a royal council and elected a *mansa,* or king, to rule the twelve kingdoms united as one.

The first kings of the Mali Kingdom belonged to the Keita clan. The first king was Latal Kalabi. Sundiata, founder of the Empire of Mali, was a later ruler. He established the new capital of the Mali Kingdom—soon to become the Mali Empire—at his birthplace, the city of Niani.

A shrine sacred to the Mande people is the Mandeblo. It is decorated with paintings that refer to the Mande creation myth and other sacred themes.

KANGABA

The original center of the Mali Kingdom was at Kangaba. The sacred shrine, the *Mandeblo*, is still there today. After Sundiata defeated the Susu, all of the Mandinka chiefs gathered at this shrine and swore allegience to Sundiata.

Every seven years Mande peoples from throughout West Africa still gather at the Mandeblo for special ceremonies. The Mandeblo is also known as the Kaaba, like the sacred cube of *Islam* that is in Mecca. This is because for several centuries a large proportion of the Mande peoples have been Muslims. The guardians of the Mandeblo sanctuary belong to the Kadesi branch of the Keita clan, which traces its descent from Sundiata.

During the ceremonies at Kangaba, symbolic signs are painted on the walls of the shrine, and performers dramatically reenact the Mande myth of creation. Griots tell sacred stories that describe the invention of speech, farming, and the crafts of blacksmithing and weaving. The latter two are regarded as the foundations of Mande civilization.

The Mande consider all creative people to be blessed individuals. Mande myths describe how the Creator, *Maa Ngala*, created the world by just speaking a few words. He intentionally left the task unfinished and gave creative people the task of completing it in the future. In Mande society, artists of all kinds play a vital role, forever forming and reforming the world.

SUNDIATA: THE HUNGERING LION

The story of Sundiata, the founder of the Mali Empire, is the most famous of all griot epics. The epic states that Sundiata's father was the handsome king Maghan Kon Fatta, whose family had ruled the Mali Kingdom for three centuries. Sundiata's mother was Sogolon Kedjou, an ugly hunchback who, before she married, could transform herself into a buffalo. When he was born, Sundiata was named Sogolon-Djata, meaning Son of the Lion and the Buffalo. He was born lame and sick, and by the age of seven Sogolon-Djata still could not walk.

The Empire of Ghana, of which the Mali Kingdom was a part, was then ruled by Sumanguru,

In the epic of Sundiata and still today, blacksmiths play an important role in West Africa.

king of the Susu. He had seized control during the chaos caused when minor kings in the empire competed for power. In the early 1200s, Sumanguru attacked Kangaba in order to capture its slaves. He spared the young Sundiata's life because the child could not walk. Before departing, however, Sumanguru insulted the Mandinka, calling them weak and spineless, just like the king's son.

HOW SUNDIATA FOUND HIS FEET

Sogolon-Djata often had to watch his mother suffer *humiliation* because of his deformed leg and her hunchback. But the day came when he could endure no more. He asked his loyal griot, Balla Fasseke, to order the royal blacksmiths to make a heavy iron rod. The rod was so heavy that six apprentices were needed to carry the iron bar to Sogolon-Djata:

> He crept on all fours and came to the iron bar. Supporting himself on his knees and one hand, with the other hand he picked up the iron bar. He grasped the bar in both hands to lean on it as a staff and lift himself into a standing position. A deathly silence had gripped all those present. With one great effort Sogolon-Djata straightened up and was on his feet—but the great bar of iron had been bowed!
>
> Then Balla Fasseke sang out the "Hymn to the Bow," striking up with his powerful voice:

> > Take your bow, Great Hunter,
> > Take your bow and let us go.
> > Take your bow, Sogolon-Djata.

When Sogolon saw her son standing, she stood dumbstruck for a moment. Then suddenly she sang these words of thanks to God, who had given her son the use of his legs:

Oh day, what a beautiful day,
Oh day, day of joy;
Allah Almighty, you never created a
    finer day.
So my son is going to walk!

After catching his breath Sogolon-Djata dropped the bar, and the crowd stood to one side. His first steps were those of a giant. Balla Fasseke fell into step behind him and, pointing his finger at Sogolon-Djata, cried:

Room, room, make room!
The lion has walked;
Hide, antelopes,
Get out of his way.

Through his courage and determination, Sogolon-Djata grew to be a brave hunter and warrior. His name was shortened to Sundiata, which means the hungering lion.

SUNDIATA WINS MALI'S FREEDOM

Sundiata became king of Mali in 1230. As king, Sundiata decided to free Mali from the brutal tyrant Sumanguru. A griot praise-song describes how Sundiata waged war on Sumanguru:

When the son of the Buffalo Woman and his army appeared, the trumpets and drums blended with the voices of the griots. The son of Sogolon was surrounded by his swift horsemen, and his horse pranced along. All eyes were fixed on the child of Mali, who shone with glory and splendor.

Raising his hand, Sundiata spoke thus: "I salute you all, sons of Mali! As long as I breathe, Mali will never be in slavery—rather death than slavery. We will be free because our ancestors were free. I am going to avenge the indignity that Mali has suffered."

Sundiata's final victory over Sumanguru took place on the plain of Kirina in 1235 when Sundiata and his army rapidly conquered a vast area. The new empire was approximately three times the size of the former Empire of Ghana.

Sundiata established an efficient system of government by appointing loyal governors to rule

Sundiata's horsemen might have looked somewhat like these West African horsemen.

distant provinces. He absorbed several lesser kings into his empire, allowing them to continue ruling their own areas while they acknowledged his authority over them. These kings paid Sundiata an annual *tribute*, a tax of produce and valuable items. After Sundiata had brought peace to the region, known as the Western Sudan, the people living there could focus on farming and trade rather than on war.

Sundiata established a new capital on the Niger River at Niani, his birthplace, although Kangaba

Kirina was one of the first towns to join Sundiata's expanding kingdom. The small structures in the foreground are used for storing grain.

remained the spiritual center of the Mali Empire. Archaeologists know the general location of Niani, but they have not yet found the exact location. The praise-songs of the griots describe Niani as a city of great wealth and power. Arabic writers described Niani's houses, which were built of clay with roofs of wood and reed, and the king's palace, which was surrounded by a wall.

The ample water supply from the Niger River allowed for farming and had been a guarantee of survival in times of drought for the Empire of

Boats are an efficient means of transport along the Niger River.

Ghana, although severe drought might have been one of the key factors in its fall. The Niger River also served as a quick transportation route, allowing trade goods to travel throughout the empire. This stimulated new trade and contributed to the wealth of the empire.

LINKS WITH THE MUSLIM WORLD

For many centuries, trade across the Sahara Desert had been conducted mainly by Berber peoples, including the Tuareg. The Berbers had been conquered in the seventh century by Arab Muslim armies that had invaded the North African coast. Over the next five hundred years, Islamic civilization led the world in learning, art, science, government, and trade.

The Berbers, however, regained control from the Arabs. Led by the Fatimids, a Muslim dynasty from Yemen, and supported by soldiers from the Western Sudan, the Berbers conquered Egypt in 969 and built their capital in Cairo, Egypt. For a time, Fatimid Berbers played a leading role in the Muslim world, which spread from North Africa to Syria and into parts of Arabia.

By the time of Sundiata's victory over Sumanguru in 1235, the Berber empire had broken into several different sections. Split by rivalries, the Berbers were unable to unify and fully control North Africa. The center of Berber power was in Tunis, located in present-day Tunisia. A web of trade routes linked Tunis with the great cities of the Sahel, including Niani, Timbuktu, Jenne, and Gao. These cities were controlled by the Empire of Mali.

The cities of the Mali Empire were populated by a mixture of peoples, including Muslims and Berber traders. Historians believe that, unlike

Boys in Timbuktu study the Koran, the holy book of Islam, and learn to write Arabic script. The ink on their wooden boards can be wiped off easily to make space for another lesson.

Sumanguru, Sundiata adopted Islam. This may have restored the confidence of the Muslim Berber merchants. They had halted business activity in the area when the Empire of Ghana was torn by war. Like Sundiata, many merchants in the Empire of Mali also converted to Islam. This made it easier for them to trade with Berbers to the north. Islamic scholarship also took root in the Empire of Mali, particularly in Timbuktu. In the countryside, however, many people still followed traditional religions.

SUNDIATA'S LEGACY

Under Sundiata, the Empire of Mali played a key role in world affairs, which were then dominated by Muslims. In fact, much of the world's economy depended on gold from the Empire of Mali.

During Sundiata's peaceful and prosperous reign, the Mali Kingdom grew into a powerful empire. The Sundiata epic ends with this tribute to Sundiata:

Some kings are powerful through their military strength. Everybody trembles before them, but when they die nothing but ill is spoken of them. Others do neither good nor ill, and when they die they are forgotten. Others are feared because they have power, but they know how to use it, and they are loved because they love justice. Sundiata belonged to this group. He was feared, but loved as well. He was the mother of Mali and gave the world peace. He made the capital of an empire out of his father's village, Niani, and Niani became the navel of the earth. . . .

Mali is eternal. To convince yourself of what I have said, go to Mali.

THE WEALTH OF THE EMPIRE

Two key factors in the success of the Mali Empire were its abundance of crops and a powerful army. Its great wealth, however, came from trade.

FARMING AND WEAVING

Farming has always been the economic foundation of the Mande world. West Africans were already cultivating crops by the end of the second millennium B.C., making them among the world's earliest farmers. Cotton, sesame, sorghum, and millet were some of the crops grown in this region. Sundiata's son, Mansa Wali, is said to have encouraged farming as his father had. By the time of his death

The ancient tradition of weaving strips of cotton cloth continues today.

in 1270, the Empire of Mali was producing a *surplus* of food for export.

One important crop was cotton, which was spun and used to weave cloth. In Mande culture, weaving is considered a divine gift, first taught to humans by spiders. Archaeological evidence suggests that Mande-speaking peoples have produced woven cotton cloth for at least one thousand years. Today, Mande men continue the ancient craft, passing on to their sons the skill of weaving long, narrow strips of cloth on horizontal looms. The woven strips can be stitched together to form a large cloth. In the past, these strips were widely used as a form of currency, and *textiles* were important trade items.

IRON

In the Sundiata epic, an iron bar is the support that allows Sundiata finally to stand on his own two feet. In a similar way, the strength of African kingdoms from A.D. 500 onward depended on iron. Iron tools and weapons produced by skilled blacksmiths equipped farmers, hunters, and warriors to feed and protect their people. The weapons used by the empire's army included iron-tipped spears, daggers, swords, and bows and arrows. Blacksmiths also carved wooden objects, such as battle clubs.

In the past as well as today, blacksmiths had a special place in Mande society. Their ability to transform rocks containing iron ore into tools by using fire, air, and water was seen as evidence of great spiritual power. Blacksmiths were so respected for their apparently supernatural abilities that

A hunter's shirt

they were also called upon to play other roles in their communities. They were doctors, spiritual guides, political advisors, and interpreters.

Blacksmiths also made hunter's shirts, which are still made and worn today. Several charms are attached to each shirt for protection and to promote success in hunting and battle. The charms include mirrors, claws, horns filled with magical medicines, and protective amulets—small leather pouches containing passages from the Koran, the holy text of the Muslims. The more charms on a shirt, the greater the hunter's physical and supernatural powers, and

Pots for sale in Mopti, in present-day Mali

the more likely he was to be a great leader. The first kings of Mali are described as hunter-warrior kings, and the Sundiata epic says that both Sundiata and his griot, Balla Fasseke, wore hunter's shirts.

Like griots and weavers, blacksmiths passed their skills and mystical knowledge from one generation to the next, and often to their sons and nephews. Mande blacksmiths' wives often were (and still are) skilled potters. They form clay from the earth into large vessels and fire them in open-air kilns. Such pots are used for carrying water, cooking, and storing food.

TRADE

Like the Empire of Ghana before it, the Empire of Mali owed its success to its strategic location in the Sahel between the gold mines in the forests of the south and the salt mines in the Sahara Desert. In Arabic, *sahel* means "shore." Since the Sahara may be thought of as a vast sea of sand, the towns on the southern edge of the desert were like ports along the shore, to which camels—the ships of the desert—brought goods.

A view of Jenne showing the distinctive flat-topped roofs

Mali's main source of wealth was its control of the Wangara gold mines and the salt mines of Taghaza. From Sundiata's reign until the 1500s, gold from the Mali Empire was the main source of gold used to make coins in the Muslim world. Europe received its gold mainly from Muslim suppliers. This meant that much of the world's currency depended on the Empire of Mali. The gold was traded for salt, which was vital to the inhabitants of the Empire of Mali.

Donkey and camel caravans brought many other goods to the cities of the empire. Among the items traded were slaves, horses, livestock, *textiles*, books, tools, wood, metal and leather goods, silver, tin, lead, ivory, perfumes, rare birds, beads, jewelry, honey, milk, rice, millet, fish, kola nuts, and shea nuts.

Trade introduced Mali's riches to Europe, Arabia, and Asia. In return, rare and precious items from these regions were brought to Mali. Scholars, poets, ambassadors, and musicians traveled together with merchants in the camel caravans. As trade flourished, camel stops grew into towns, which were joined together by a vast network of trade routes.

4 MANSA MUSA

Sundiata died an accidental death in 1255. His son, Mansa Wali, ruled until his death in 1270.

It is said that one of the heirs to the throne, a great-grandson of Sundiata named Mansa Muhammad, showed no interest in the throne. He was determined to explore the Atlantic Ocean by sailing west. Sometime between 1300 and 1310 he set out with a large fleet. After a long time he returned with the strange story that his fleet had encountered a river with a strong current flowing into the sea, which had sunk all the ships but his. Some scholars believe that Mansa Muhammad may have succeeded in crossing the Atlantic Ocean.

After Mansa Wali's death, the Empire of Mali was plunged into uncertainty as several possible leaders struggled for power. In 1307, a grandson of one of Sundiata's sisters took the throne. His name was Musa, which means "Moses" in Arabic.

During the reign of Mansa Musa, who became one of Africa's most famous kings, the size of the Mali Empire doubled and its volume of trade tripled. New gold mines were discovered farther to the east. Sagaman-dir, Mansa Musa's army commander, captured Gao, the capital of the neighboring city-state of Songhay. This military victory gave Mali control of the copper mines of Tadmekka. Mansa Musa is reported to have said that copper was the main source of his wealth.

ISLAM

In 1312, motivated in part by a desire to strengthen trade links with the Arab world, Mansa Musa made Islam the official religion of the Mali Empire. He welcomed Arabs to his kingdom. In Mali, the *ulama,* meaning the learned, who were the officials and teachers of Islam, became politically powerful in the cities. At the same time, Mansa Musa respected the traditional African religions followed by most of his subjects in the countryside. He did not force people to convert to Islam.

In about 1353, twenty years after Mansa Musa's death, an Arabic writer from Morocco named Ibn Battuta spent about fifty days in Niani. He was impressed by how Islam and ancient African religious practices blended peacefully in Mali. As an example of this peace, he described a celebration during which griots gave a traditional African performance for their Muslim emperor. The griots, disguised as birds and wearing feathered costumes and beaked masks, asked the *mansa* to remember and imitate the good deeds of his ancestors so that his own actions would bring him eternal glory.

MANSA MUSA'S HAJJ

In 1324 Mansa Musa set off across the desert with an enormous *entourage*. He was following a Muslim obligation that those who are able should make the *hajj*, a pilgrimage to the holy city of Mecca. It was to be one the most famous journeys ever undertaken in world history.

Estimates of the number of people who accom-

The Kaaba in Mecca is the most sacred site of Muslim worship. Every year more than a million Muslims make the hajj and pray at the Kaaba.

panied him vary from 8,000 to 60,000. Among these were many of the empire's princes, chiefs, and military leaders. This was, in part, to prevent them from sowing unrest in his absence. He also took his wife, together with her five hundred attendants.

They crossed the desert, taking with them a huge herd of animals for transport and food. Five hundred slaves each carried a 6-pound (2.7-kg) staff of gold. Another 30,000 pounds (14,000 kg) of gold were loaded onto one hundred camels. One hundred camels carried food, clothing, and supplies.

Mansa Musa's caravan amazed everyone who saw it. Egyptian author al-Umari described it as "a lavish display of power and wealth that was unprecedented in its size and pageantry." In keeping with a teaching of Islam that the rich must share their wealth with the poor, Mansa Musa gave away a great deal of gold on his journey. In fact, he gave away so much gold in Cairo that it lost its rarity, and the price of gold dropped. It is said that prices in Cairo were so disrupted that it took more than twelve years for Egypt's economy to recover from Mansa Musa's visit.

Mansa Musa's pilgrimage cemented relationships with Egypt and the Muslim world to the east. It also encouraged new immigrants and visitors to the cities of Mali. While in Mecca, Mansa Musa met Abu Ishaq es-Saheli, an Arab architect and poet from southern Spain. He returned to Mali with

Architect Abu Ishaq es-Saheli, whom Mansa Musa met in Mecca, is credited with having developed West Africa's distinctive mosque design. The Grand Mosque of Jenne was built in 1905, following a traditional style.

Mansa Musa and designed for him several royal palaces and the famous Sankore mosque in Timbuktu.

Timbuktu was an important center of trade and learning during this period. The city had a large international population of merchants, artisans, and scholars, most of whom were Muslims. Sankore University, with its famous libraries of Arabic texts, was located there. It was in the universities of the Muslim world such as Timbuktu that the classical texts of ancient Greece and Rome were preserved. They had been destroyed in Europe and were only reintroduced there during the Renaissance.

THE EMPEROR'S COURT

Historian al-Umari reported in 1325 that Mansa Musa held court on a wide balcony. He sat on a great wooden throne placed between elephant tusks and wore trousers of sewn cloth strips in an exclusive pattern. Mansa Musa was surrounded by his weapons, all made of gold, and a dozen Turkish slaves, one of whom shaded him with a silk umbrella.

Ibn Battuta visited the court of Mali a few

The emperor controlled many lesser kings throughout the empire. They may have dressed in a manner similar to this Tucolor king. On the basis of descriptions, Mansa Musa's dress was even more impressive.

decades later. His impressions of Mali appear in the book *Ibn Battuta in Black Africa* by Said Hamdun and Noël King.

Ibn Battuta describes the emperor of Mali receiving his subjects while seated on silk pillows:

> The soldiers, district governors, pages, and others are seated outside the place of audience in a broad street that has trees in it. Each commander has his followers with him with their spears, bows, drums, and bugles made of elephant tusks. Their musical instruments are made of reeds and calabashes, and they beat them with sticks and produce a wonderful sound. Each commander has a quiver, which he places between his shoulders. He holds his bow in his hand and is mounted on a mare. Some of his men are on foot, and some are on mounts.

Ibn Battuta found that the women of Mali were treated with more respect than the men. They had far greater freedom than other Muslim women. Though these women were devout Muslims, they neither wore veils nor covered their breasts. Ibn Battuta found the people of Mali to be exceptionally peaceful and just. He wrote:

> The king pardons no one who is guilty . . . There is complete and general safety throughout the land. The traveler here has no more reason than the man who stays at home to fear brigands, thieves, or ravishers . . . The inhabitants do not confiscate the goods of any North Africans who may die in their country, not even when these consist of large treasures. On the contrary, they deposit these goods with a trustworthy man until those who have the right to the goods present themselves and take possession.

Mansa Musa's reign coincided with the peak of Muslim world domination, and Mali played a vital role in the economy of that world.

But statements by Muslim writers such as Ibn Battuta show that the Empire of Mali was a most impressive place for many reasons. Its universities, good government and legal system, the freedom and

This door in Timbuktu features a carved frame and is held together with ornamental metal studs and clasps. It illustrates the architectural and artistic skills for which the Empire of Mali was famous.

respect given to women, and its architecture, arts, and crafts all made it remarkable.

5 THE DECLINE

After Mansa Musa's death, his son, Maghan, became king. During his four-year reign, Timbuktu was raided and burned by warriors from the east. This demonstrated to others how vulnerable the Empire of Mali was to attack. In the next century the empire was attacked from all sides.

By 1433, Timbuktu had been captured and was controlled by Berbers. By the mid-1400s, Mali had lost its northern provinces to the Tuareg Berbers, losing control over the Saharan trade. In the west, the Tucolor and Wolof city-states revolted against Mali. Mali's southern trade routes and market towns were attacked by Mossi cavalry between

The Mali Empire was composed of many different peoples, some of whom revolted against Mali's control. Seen here is a Fulani nomad from the Sahel. He is dressed for an annual courtship dance during which young women select the men of their choice.

1430 and 1483. In the eastern region of Gao, however, the Songhay Kingdom, independent since the late 1300s, was gathering force. Soon it would emerge as the next great West African empire.

EUROPE

As the Empire of Mali peaked and then began to decline, Arab world power was on the decrease. European power grew.

Europe's awareness of Africa had grown steadily. From the eleventh century onward, Berbers and Arabs had great influence in Spain. They intermarried with Spaniards and reintroduced much of the knowledge that had been lost to Europe during its Middle Ages. From the 1200s onward, more and more Africans were sold into slavery in European cities such as Genoa, Naples, and Barcelona.

In the fourteenth century, Europeans were eager to make direct contact with the wealthy Empire of Mali rather than having to buy gold and other African goods from Muslim traders. The first European map of West Africa, which was drawn in

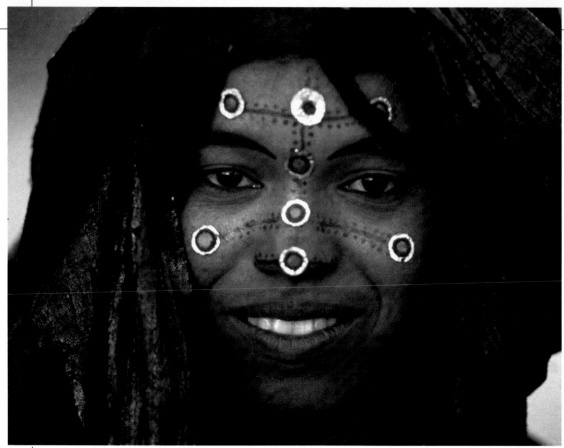

A Berber from the Sahel

1375 for Charles V of France by a Majorcan map-maker, shows how large Mansa Musa loomed in the European imagination. Wearing a gold crown and holding a golden staff, Mansa Musa's figure dominates the map. In his outstretched hand he holds a gold nugget; a trader approaches on a camel. It is possibly because of Mansa Musa that European artists in the fourteenth century were inspired to represent one of the Three Wise Men in the New Testament as an African king.

By the fifteenth century, some Europeans were in direct contact with the Empire of Mali. One example is Anselme d'Isaguier, a noble trader and politician from Toulouse, France. He married Salam Casais, the daughter of a Songhay chief and a member of a wealthy, influential family in Gao, which was then controlled by Mali. Salam Casais traveled back to France with him accompanied by six Malian attendants. They crossed the Sahara and then sailed from North Africa to France. In 1413 they finally arrived in France. One of Salam Casais's companions was Aben Ali, a medical doctor. He became so famous in France for his skills that in 1419 he treated Prince Charles, heir to the throne of France.

In the mid-1400s, Florence, Italy, was the leading center of commerce and culture in southern Europe. In 1469, a Florentine bank sent Benedetto Dei, an agent of the Portinari company in Florence, to Timbuktu to negotiate a trade agreement with the *mansa*. Europe was finally in direct contact with the Empire of Mali.

A detail of a map created in 1375 shows Mansa Musa seated, lower right, with a gold nugget in his hand. It demonstrates the importance of Mansa Musa in the European view of Africa.

THE ATLANTIC TRADE

The Portuguese were the first Europeans to sail around the bulge of West Africa, in 1471. The voyage was made possible when the Portuguese adopted a type of sail, the *lateen*, that the Arabs had been using for centuries. The Portuguese, rapidly followed by other European powers, established trading posts along the African coast. Europeans could now obtain gold, slaves, and African products by stopping at these Atlantic ports. There was no longer a need to trade with Muslim merchants or hazard the crossing of the Sahara Desert. Though some trade still flowed across the Sahara (and continues today), the Atlantic trade grew rapidly and drained the lifeblood from the great cities of the Sahel. The African peoples along the Atlantic coast grew wealthy from trading directly with Europeans.

European colonization of the Americas also affected Africa. After Europeans found new sources of gold in the Americas, African gold became less important than the African slave trade. In addition, Europeans wanted large numbers of slaves to work the plantations they established in the Americas.

THE FALL OF MALI

Like the earlier Empire of Ghana, the Empire of Mali gradually disintegrated because of internal conflict and attack by outsiders. The Empire of Songhay later rose in its place. Greatly reduced in power, Mali maintained control of the gold fields of Bambuk until the end of the 1500s, when the Empire of Songhay also began to collapse.

In 1599, Mansa Mamudu was defeated at the gates of Jenne by Moroccans. He fled to Niani on horseback, signaling the end of the Mali Empire.

THE LEGACY OF MALI

Though Mali had declined, the fame of its wealth, power, and cultural achievements never faded from memory. Tales of Mansa Musa's fabulous hajj have been told in Africa and the Muslim world for generations.

Today, the Western Sudan is divided into many countries, most of which were ruled by France until their independence in 1960. The modern country of Mali, which includes the cities of Timbuktu, Gao, and Jenne, was named in honor of the Empire of Mali.

Griots sometimes use drums as they recount the glorious history of the Empire of Mali.

The glorious past of Mali continues to inspire popular musicians, filmmakers, writers, and artists in West Africa. Griots still recount the achievements of the Empire of Mali, though some of them feel that this great history is now being overwhelmed by the problems of modern life. However, as long as the griots and modern musicians continue to sing about the Empire of Mali, each new generation will learn about one of the greatest empires the world has ever seen.

TIMELINE

A.D.	1076	Almoravid Berbers defeat Empire of Ghana
	early 1200s	Sumanguru rules the fragmented Empire of Ghana and attacks Kangaba but spares Sundiata's life
	1230	Sundiata becomes king of Mali
	1235	Sundiata conquers Sumanguru's army
	1235–1255	Sundiata builds Empire of Mali; gold from Mali becomes source of gold for Muslim and European currency
	1255–1270	Reign of Mansa Wali, Sundiata's son; expansion of empire; growth in agricultural production
	1307–1332	Reign of Mansa Musa; empire doubles in size and trade triples; Muslim influence worldwide increases
	1312	Mansa Musa makes Islam the official religion of Mali
	1324	Mansa Musa begins his pilgrimage to Mecca
	1332	Mansa Maghan begins to rule; Timbuktu is later raided
	c. 1375–1400	Songhay asserts independence
	c. 1400–1480	Empire of Mali pressed by the Songhay and Tuareg; northern province breaks away; Jenne and Timbuktu assert independence; decline of Mali's power; empire raided by the Mossi
	1471	Portuguese arrive in West Africa
	1493-1495	An ambassador of the Portuguese king visits Mansa Mamudu
	c. 1590-1600	Collapse of the Empire of Mali

GLOSSARY

city-state self-governing state consisting of a city and its surrounding territory

entourage group of persons who accompany someone

griot West African storyteller who passes on the history of a people through epics

hajj Islamic pilgrimage to the holy city of Mecca

humiliation state of being lowered in status in one's own eyes

Islam religion that teaches that Allah is the one God

kora stringed instrument used by griots in Mali

lateen triangular cloth sail

Maa Ngala Creator of the Mande people

Mandeblo sacred shrine of the Mande people

Mandinka people of West Africa who built the Mali Empire

mansa king elected to rule the twelve Mandinka kingdoms

negotiator one who settles a matter with others by discussion and compromise

Sahel region lying between the Sahara Desert and the forest lands to the south

sect one branch of a religious belief

surplus an extra amount of something

textiles fabrics

tribute payment in money or goods required of a country by the stronger ruler of another country

FOR FURTHER READING

Franck, Irene M., and David Brownstone. *Across Africa and Arabia.* New York, Oxford: Facts on File, 1991.

McKissack, Frederick, and Patricia McKissack. *The Royal Kingdoms of Ghana, Mali, and Songhay.* New York: Henry Holt and Company, 1994.

National Museum of African Art. *The Art of West African Kingdoms.* Washington, DC: National Museum of African Art, Smithsonian Institution Press, 1987.

Wisniewski, David. *Sundiata: Lion King of Mali.* New York: Clarion, 1992.

FOR ADVANCED READERS

Bovill, Edward William. *The Golden Trade of the Moors.* Princeton: Markus Wiener Publishers, 1995.

Hamdun, Said, and Noël King. *Ibn Battuta in Black Africa.* Princeton: Markus Wiener Publishers, 1994 (1975).

Levtzion, Nehemia. *Ancient Ghana and Mali.* New York: Holmes and Meier Publishers, 1980.

Niane, D. T. *Sundiata: An Epic of Old Mali.* Translated by G. D. Pickett. Essex, England: Longman, 1965 (1960).

WEB SITES

Due to the changeable nature of the Internet, sites appear and disappear very quickly. Internet addresses must be entered with capital and lowercase letters exactly as they appear.

Detroit Institute of Arts—African, Oceanic, and New World Cultures home page: http://www.dia.org/galleries/aonwcindex.html

Detroit News—Mali's vanishing heritage: http://detnews.com/menu/stories/17508.htm

Seydou Keita's photographs from Mali: http://zonezero.com/exposiciones/fotografos/keita

INDEX

ABOUT THE AUTHOR

Carol Thompson received a Master's degree in art history from the University of Iowa in 1988. From 1987 to 1996 she was Curator for Education and Associate Curator at The Museum for African Art in New York City. She has taught at New York University, the Fashion Institute of Technology, Pace University, and City College of New York. She is a frequent public speaker on the art and culture of Africa and the African diaspora, past and present. Her interest in African art has taken her to Burkina Faso, Ghana, Togo, Malawi, and to Mali, where she presented a paper on textiles at the international conference of the Mande Studies Association (MANSA) in 1993. She is currently completing a Ph.D. in Performance Studies at New York University's Tisch School of the Arts.